THE SALES OF THE MIND WITH AI: UNLEASHING COGNITIVE POWER IN SELLING

BY

HENRY E. PARKINS

1

COPYRIGHT PAGE

TABLE OF CONTENTS

3

INTRODUCTION

In the dynamic landscape of sales, success hinges not only on the products or services being offered but also on the intricate interplay of human cognition and technological innovation. "The Sales of the Mind with AI: Unleashing Cognitive Power in Selling" delves into the revolutionary fusion of cognitive science and artificial intelligence (AI) reshaping the sales domain.

In this era of rapid digital transformation, understanding the nuances of human behavior and leveraging cutting-edge AI technologies have become pivotal in driving sales performance and fostering sustainable growth. This book serves as a comprehensive guide for sales professionals, leaders, and enthusiasts alike, navigating the complex intersection of psychology, technology, and commerce.

At its core, this book explores the profound implications of harnessing cognitive power and AI advancements to optimize sales strategies, enhance customer relationships, and unlock untapped potentials within sales organizations. By bridging the gap between human intuition and computational intelligence, we embark on a journey towards redefining the art and science of selling.

Through insightful analysis, practical insights, and real-world examples, "The Sales of the Mind with AI" equips readers with the knowledge and tools necessary to thrive in an increasingly competitive marketplace. From understanding the intricacies of the sales mindset to implementing AI-driven solutions, this book offers a roadmap for driving sustainable business growth and achieving sales excellence in the digital age.

AI in Sales

Artificial Intelligence (AI) in sales refers to the integration of advanced computational algorithms, machine learning techniques, and cognitive technologies to automate, optimize, and augment various aspects of the sales process. At its essence, AI In sales empowers organizations to leverage vast amounts of data, glean actionable insights, and personalize interactions with customers and prospects to drive revenue growth and enhance overall sales performance.

AI in sales encompasses a diverse array of applications, including but not limited to predictive analytics, sales forecasting, lead scoring, customer segmentation, chatbots, natural language processing (NLP), and recommendation engines. By harnessing the power of AI, sales teams can streamline repetitive tasks, identify patterns and trends, anticipate customer needs, and deliver hyper-personalized experiences at scale.

Moreover, AI in sales transcends traditional boundaries, enabling organizations to adapt and respond dynamically to evolving market conditions, consumer preferences, and competitive landscapes. Through continuous learning and adaptation, AI-powered sales solutions empower businesses to stay agile, resilient, and customer-centric in an increasingly complex and interconnected global marketplace.

In "The Sales of the Mind with AI," we explore the multifaceted dimensions of AI in sales, delving into its transformative potential, ethical considerations, and practical implications for sales professionals and organizations. By demystifying the complexities of AI and elucidating its strategic relevance in the sales domain, this book seeks to equip readers with the knowledge and insights needed to harness the full potential of AI and unleash cognitive power in selling.

Importance of Cognitive Power in Selling

In the realm of sales, success is not merely contingent upon product knowledge or persuasive techniques; it is profoundly influenced by the intricate workings of human cognition. Cognitive power, encompassing a range of mental processes such as perception, attention, memory, decision-making, and emotional intelligence, plays a pivotal role in shaping sales interactions, driving customer engagement, and ultimately, closing deals.

One of the fundamental aspects of cognitive power in selling lies in understanding the psychology of human behavior. Sales professionals who possess insights into customer motivations, preferences, and pain points are better equipped to tailor their approach, establish rapport, and build meaningful connections with prospects. By leveraging cognitive empathy and active listening skills, sales professionals can empathize with customer needs, address objections, and offer solutions that resonate on a personal level.

Furthermore, cognitive power empowers sales professionals to navigate the complexities of decision-making processes effectively. By tapping into principles of cognitive psychology, such as prospect theory and behavioral economics, sales professionals can influence customer perceptions, frame value propositions, and facilitate decision-making in their favor. Understanding the biases, heuristics, and cognitive shortcuts that influence human judgment enables sales professionals to craft persuasive arguments, mitigate objections, and guide prospects through the sales funnel with greater efficiency and efficacy.

Moreover, cognitive power plays a crucial role in fostering resilience and adaptability in the face of uncertainty and adversity. Sales professionals who possess cognitive flexibility, creative problem-solving skills, and emotional intelligence are better equipped to navigate challenging situations, overcome objections, and pivot strategies in response to changing market dynamics or customer needs. By cultivating a growth mindset and embracing continuous learning, sales professionals can leverage cognitive power to drive innovation, foster collaboration, and maintain a competitive edge in today's dynamic business environment.

In "The Sales of the Mind with AI," we explore the symbiotic relationship between cognitive power and artificial intelligence, elucidating how advancements in cognitive technologies are revolutionizing sales practices and reshaping the future of selling. By harnessing the collective power of human intuition and computational intelligence, sales professionals can unlock new opportunities, optimize performance, and elevate the art and science of selling to unprecedented heights.

Overview of the Book

"The Sales of the Mind with AI: Unleashing Cognitive Power in Selling" embarks on a transformative journey at the intersection of human cognition and artificial intelligence, illuminating the dynamic landscape of modern selling and the profound impact of cognitive technologies on sales practices.

Divided into meticulously crafted chapters, this book serves as a comprehensive guide for sales professionals, leaders, and enthusiasts seeking to harness the transformative potential of cognitive power and AI in driving sales excellence and fostering sustainable growth.

The journey begins with an exploration of the fundamental principles underlying the sales mindset, delving into the psychology of human behavior, emotional intelligence, and the art of persuasion. Readers are introduced to the foundational elements of cognitive power in selling, empowering them to cultivate empathy, resilience, and adaptability in their sales endeavors.

As the narrative unfolds, readers are introduced to the transformative capabilities of artificial intelligence in sales. From predictive analytics and customer segmentation to personalized recommendations and sales automation, AI emerges as a powerful ally in optimizing sales processes, enhancing customer experiences, and unlocking new opportunities for revenue growth.

Navigating the ethical and moral considerations inherent in AI-driven sales practices, the book offers insights into the responsible use of technology, ensuring fairness, transparency, and integrity in sales interactions. Through thought-provoking discussions and real-world examples, readers gain a deeper understanding of the ethical implications of AI in sales and the imperative of upholding ethical standards in the pursuit of commercial success.

The book also provides practical guidance on implementing AI strategies within sales organizations, addressing challenges related to change management, talent development, and organizational readiness. By equipping readers with the knowledge, tools, and best practices needed to navigate the complexities of AI adoption, the book empowers sales professionals to embrace innovation, drive organizational change, and stay ahead of the curve in an increasingly competitive marketplace.

Through insightful case studies, examples, and future trends, "The Sales of the Mind with AI" offers a glimpse into the transformative potential of cognitive power and AI in shaping the future of selling. As readers embark on this illuminating journey, they are invited to explore the limitless possibilities of human ingenuity and technological innovation, revolutionizing the way we sell, connect, and succeed in the digital age

CHAPTER 1

UNDERSTANDING

THE SALES MINDSET

In the intricate dance of sales, success often hinges not just on the product or service being offered, but also on the intricate workings of the human mind. The sales mindset encompasses a complex interplay of psychological factors, emotional intelligence, and strategic thinking, all of which are instrumental in forging meaningful connections with customers, navigating objections, and ultimately, closing deals.

At its core, the sales mindset is rooted in empathy and understanding. Sales professionals who possess a deep understanding of human behavior, motivations, and aspirations are better equipped to forge authentic connections with customers, earning their trust and loyalty in the process. By cultivating empathy and active listening skills, sales professionals can uncover latent needs, address pain points, and offer tailored solutions that resonate on a personal level.

Emotional intelligence, another cornerstone of the sales mindset, enables sales professionals to navigate the complexities of human emotions with finesse and grace. By recognizing and managing their own emotions, as well as those of their customers, sales professionals can foster rapport, diffuse tension, and build long-lasting relationships based on mutual trust and respect. Moreover, emotional intelligence empowers sales professionals to adapt their communication style, tailor their approach, and effectively influence customer perceptions, ultimately driving favorable outcomes.

Strategic thinking is also central to the sales mindset, empowering sales professionals to anticipate challenges, identify opportunities, and chart a course toward success. By adopting a strategic mindset, sales professionals can analyze market trends, assess competitive landscapes, and identify areas for growth and innovation. Strategic thinking also entails a willingness to embrace change, experiment with new approaches, and pivot strategies in response to evolving customer needs and market dynamics.

In "The Sales of the Mind with AI," we delve into the intricacies of the sales mindset, exploring its multifaceted dimensions and practical implications for sales professionals and organizations. Through thought-provoking insights, real-world examples, and actionable strategies, we empower readers to cultivate a sales mindset grounded in empathy, emotional intelligence, and strategic thinking. By harnessing the power of the human mind, sales professionals can unlock new opportunities, drive meaningful connections, and achieve unparalleled success in the ever-evolving landscape of sales.

Psychology of Sales

The psychology of sales delves into the intricate workings of the human mind and behavior, shedding light on the underlying motivations, biases, and decision-making processes that shape customer interactions and purchasing decisions. By understanding the psychological principles at play, sales professionals can effectively influence customer perceptions, anticipate objections, and cultivate lasting relationships that drive sales success.

One of the foundational principles of the psychology of sales is the concept of persuasion. Drawing from theories of social psychology and persuasion, sales professionals can leverage various persuasive techniques and communication strategies to effectively engage with customers and guide them through the sales process. From the reciprocity principle to social proof and scarcity, understanding the principles of persuasion empowers sales professionals to craft compelling messages, overcome objections, and ultimately, close deals.

Furthermore, the psychology of sales encompasses the art of active listening and empathy. By actively listening to customer concerns, understanding their needs, and empathizing with their experiences, sales professionals can build rapport and establish trust, laying the groundwork for meaningful relationships built on mutual understanding and respect. Empathy allows sales professionals to see the world from the customer's perspective, identify pain points, and offer tailored solutions that address their unique challenges and aspirations.

Closely related to empathy is the concept of emotional intelligence, which plays a pivotal role in sales success. Emotional intelligence encompasses the ability to recognize, understand, and manage one's own emotions, as well as those of others. By cultivating emotional intelligence, sales professionals can navigate challenging situations, diffuse tension, and build rapport with customers, fostering trust and loyalty in the process.

Moreover, the psychology of sales sheds light on the importance of framing and context in shaping customer perceptions. By framing products or services in a positive light and emphasizing their value proposition, sales professionals can influence customer perceptions and increase the likelihood of purchase. Understanding the impact of framing allows sales professionals to position offerings in a way that resonates with customer needs and preferences, driving sales success.

In "The Sales of the Mind with AI," we delve into the intricacies of the psychology of sales, exploring its practical applications and implications for sales professionals leveraging cognitive power and artificial intelligence. By understanding the psychological principles that underpin customer behavior, sales professionals can unlock new opportunities, drive meaningful connections, and achieve unparalleled success in the ever-evolving landscape of sales.

Emotional Intelligence in Selling

In the fast-paced and often emotionally charged world of sales, emotional intelligence (EI) emerges as a cornerstone for building meaningful connections, fostering trust, and driving successful outcomes. Emotional intelligence encompasses a range of skills and competencies that enable sales professionals to recognize, understand, and manage their own emotions, as well as the emotions of others, in order to navigate complex interpersonal dynamics and cultivate authentic relationships with customers.

One of the key components of emotional intelligence in selling is self-awareness. Sales professionals who possess self-awareness are attuned to their own emotions, strengths, and weaknesses, allowing them to recognize how their thoughts and feelings influence their behavior and interactions with others. By cultivating self-awareness, sales professionals can identify areas for growth, manage stress effectively, and project authenticity and confidence in their interactions with customers.

Self-regulation is another critical aspect of emotional intelligence in selling. Sales professionals who exhibit self-regulation are able to manage their emotions and impulses in challenging situations, maintaining composure and professionalism even in the face of rejection or adversity. By practicing self-regulation, sales professionals can navigate objections, diffuse tension, and maintain a positive attitude, thereby enhancing their ability to build rapport and earn the trust of customers.

21

Empathy, a core component of emotional intelligence, is essential for building genuine connections with customers. Sales professionals who demonstrate empathy are able to understand and resonate with the emotions, perspectives, and experiences of their customers, fostering trust and rapport in the process. By listening actively, validating customer concerns, and demonstrating genuine concern for their well-being, sales professionals can cultivate empathetic connections that lay the foundation for long-lasting relationships and repeat business.

Social skills round out the repertoire of emotional intelligence in selling, enabling sales professionals to navigate interpersonal relationships with finesse and grace. Sales professionals with strong social skills excel at building rapport, communicating effectively, and influencing others in a positive and persuasive manner. By leveraging social skills, sales professionals can adapt their communication style to suit the preferences and personalities of different customers, fostering collaboration and cooperation throughout the sales process.

Developing a Sales Mindset

In the fast-paced and competitive world of sales, success is not solely determined by product knowledge or persuasive techniques; it is profoundly influenced by the development of a resilient and strategic sales mindset. A sales mindset encompasses a unique blend of attitudes, beliefs, and behaviors that empower sales professionals to navigate challenges, seize opportunities, and drive meaningful outcomes in their interactions with customers and prospects.

One of the foundational elements of developing a sales mindset is cultivating a growth-oriented perspective. Sales professionals who embrace a growth mindset understand that abilities and skills can be developed through dedication, effort, and continuous learning. By adopting a mindset focused on growth and improvement, sales professionals are better equipped to overcome obstacles, learn from failures, and persist in the face of adversity, ultimately positioning themselves for long-term success.

Furthermore, developing a sales mindset involves cultivating resilience and grit in the face of rejection and setbacks. Sales professionals who possess resilience are able to bounce back from disappointments, setbacks, and failures with a renewed sense of determination and perseverance. By reframing challenges as opportunities for growth and learning, sales professionals can develop the resilience needed to navigate the highs and lows of the sales profession with grace and resilience.

Strategic thinking is also central to developing a sales mindset. Sales professionals who think strategically are able to anticipate trends, identify opportunities, and chart a course toward success. By analyzing market dynamics, understanding customer needs, and aligning their actions with organizational goals, sales professionals can make informed decisions and prioritize activities that drive maximum impact and value for their customers and organizations.

Moreover, developing a sales mindset entails fostering a customer-centric approach to selling. Sales professionals who prioritize the needs, preferences, and experiences of their customers are better positioned to build trust, foster loyalty, and drive long-term relationships. By actively listening to customer feedback, soliciting input, and delivering value-added solutions, sales professionals can cultivate a customer-centric mindset that sets them apart in a crowded marketplace.

CHAPTER 2

LEVERAGING ARTIFICIAL INTELLIGENCE IN SALES

Introduction to AI in Sales

Welcome to the forefront of the sales revolution, where the fusion of human ingenuity and artificial intelligence (AI) is reshaping the landscape of commerce and transforming the way organizations engage with customers, optimize processes, and drive revenue growth. In this era of digital disruption, AI has emerged as a powerful catalyst for innovation, empowering sales professionals to unlock new levels of efficiency, effectiveness, and insight in their pursuit of sales excellence.

At its essence, AI in sales represents the convergence of advanced computational algorithms, machine learning techniques, and cognitive technologies that enable organizations to harness the power of data-driven insights, predictive analytics, and personalized engagement strategies to drive meaningful connections and achieve unprecedented levels of sales performance.

The journey into AI in sales begins with a fundamental shift in mindset a recognition of the transformative potential of AI to augment human capabilities, enhance decision-making, and drive strategic outcomes in the sales domain. By embracing AI-driven technologies, sales professionals can transcend traditional boundaries, anticipate customer needs, and deliver hyper-personalized experiences that resonate with individual preferences and interests, ultimately fostering deeper connections and driving customer loyalty.

One of the key pillars of AI in sales lies in predictive analytics and forecasting. By analyzing vast amounts of historical data and identifying patterns and trends, AI algorithms can generate actionable insights into customer behavior, market dynamics, and sales performance, enabling organizations to make informed decisions, allocate resources effectively, and capitalize on emerging opportunities in real-time.

Moreover, AI enables sales professionals to automate routine tasks and streamline workflows, freeing up valuable time and resources for high-value activities such as relationship-building, problem-solving, and strategic planning. From lead generation and qualification to sales forecasting and performance tracking, AI-powered automation tools empower sales teams to focus on what matters most—cultivating meaningful connections, delivering exceptional value, and driving sustainable growth.

Furthermore, AI-driven technologies such as natural language processing (NLP), sentiment analysis, and conversational AI are revolutionizing the way organizations engage with customers across various touchpoints, from email communications and social media interactions to live chat and customer service inquiries. By understanding and responding to customer needs in real-time, AI-powered solutions enable organizations to deliver personalized experiences, resolve issues proactively, and build lasting relationships that drive long-term success.

Applications of AI in Sales Processes

Predictive Analytics and Forecasting: AI-powered predictive analytics enable sales professionals to forecast future sales trends, identify high-value opportunities, and anticipate customer needs with greater accuracy. By analyzing historical data and identifying patterns and correlations, AI algorithms empower sales teams to make informed decisions, allocate resources effectively, and optimize sales strategies for maximum impact.

Lead Scoring and Prioritization: AI-driven lead scoring models leverage data analytics and machine learning techniques to evaluate and prioritize leads based on their likelihood to convert into customers. By analyzing demographic, behavioral, and firmographic data, AI algorithms enable sales teams to focus their efforts on leads with the highest potential for conversion, improving efficiency and driving higher sales outcomes.

Personalized Recommendations and Content:

AI-powered recommendation engines analyze customer behavior, preferences, and purchase history to deliver personalized product recommendations and content tailored to individual interests and needs. By leveraging machine learning algorithms, sales professionals can engage customers with relevant offers and content, enhancing the overall customer experience and driving higher conversion rates.

Sales Process Automation:

AI-driven sales automation tools streamline repetitive tasks and administrative processes, allowing sales professionals to focus on high-value activities such as relationship-building and strategic planning. From automated email sequences and follow-up reminders to scheduling appointments and updating CRM records, AI-powered automation improves productivity, efficiency, and consistency across the sales process.

Customer Segmentation and Targeting:

AI-powered customer segmentation techniques analyze large datasets to identify distinct customer segments based on demographic, behavioral, and psychographic attributes. By segmenting customers into homogenous groups, sales professionals can tailor their messaging and targeting strategies to resonate with specific audience segments, increasing the effectiveness of marketing campaigns and sales initiatives.

Sales Performance Tracking and Optimization:

AI-driven analytics platforms provide real-time insights into sales performance metrics, such as conversion rates, win rates, and sales cycle length. By tracking key performance indicators and identifying areas for improvement, sales professionals can optimize their sales processes, refine their strategies, and drive continuous improvement across the organization.

Virtual Assistants and Chatbots:

AI-powered virtual assistants and chatbots provide personalized support and assistance to customers throughout the sales journey. By leveraging natural language processing (NLP) and machine learning algorithms, virtual assistants can answer customer inquiries, provide product recommendations, and facilitate transactions in real-time, enhancing the overall customer experience and driving higher levels of engagement and satisfaction.

In "The Sales of the Mind with AI," we explore the diverse applications of AI in sales processes, providing practical insights and actionable strategies for sales professionals and organizations seeking to leverage the power of AI to drive sales excellence and achieve competitive advantage in the digital age.

Benefits of AI in Sales

Enhanced Sales Efficiency: AI-powered automation streamlines repetitive tasks and administrative processes, allowing sales professionals to focus their time and energy on high-value activities such as relationship-building, strategic planning, and customer engagement. By automating routine tasks such as data entry, lead qualification, and follow-up communication, AI enables sales teams to operate more efficiently and effectively, driving productivity and performance across the organization.

Improved Sales Forecasting and Predictability:

AI-driven predictive analytics leverage advanced algorithms to analyze historical sales data, identify patterns and trends, and forecast future sales outcomes with greater accuracy. By providing sales professionals with actionable insights into market dynamics, customer behavior, and sales performance, AI enables organizations to make informed decisions, allocate resources effectively, and optimize sales strategies for maximum impact and profitability.

Personalized Customer Experiences:

AI-powered recommendation engines analyze customer data, preferences, and behaviors to deliver personalized product recommendations, content, and offers tailored to individual interests and needs. By understanding

33

customer preferences and anticipating their needs, AI enables sales professionals to create more meaningful and relevant interactions with customers, fostering trust, loyalty, and long-term relationships.

Enhanced Lead Generation and Qualification:

AI-driven lead scoring models evaluate and prioritize leads based on their likelihood to convert into customers, enabling sales teams to focus their efforts on high-value opportunities with the greatest potential for success. By leveraging machine learning algorithms to analyze demographic, behavioral, and firmographic data, AI enables organizations to identify and engage with prospects at the right time, with the right message, and through the right channels, maximizing conversion rates and revenue growth.

Real-Time Insights and Decision-Making:

AI-powered analytics platforms provide real-time insights into sales performance metrics, customer interactions, and market trends, enabling sales professionals to make data-driven decisions and adapt their strategies in real-time. By tracking key performance indicators and identifying areas for improvement, AI empowers sales teams to optimize their processes, refine their approaches, and drive continuous improvement across the organization.

Scalability and Adaptability: AI-driven sales solutions are inherently scalable and adaptable, allowing organizations to easily scale their operations and adapt to changing market conditions, customer preferences, and competitive landscapes. By leveraging cloud-based platforms and scalable infrastructure, AI enables organizations to quickly deploy new features, integrate with existing systems, and expand their sales capabilities to meet evolving business needs and opportunities.

Competitive Advantage: By embracing AI in sales, organizations gain a competitive advantage in the marketplace by differentiating themselves through innovation, efficiency, and customer-centricity. By leveraging AI to deliver personalized experiences, optimize processes, and drive sales performance, organizations can position themselves as

leaders in their industries, attract and retain top talent, and drive sustainable growth and success in the digital age.

CHAPTER 3

ENHANCING SALES PERFORMANCE WITH COGNITIVE TECHNOLOGIES

In the dynamic landscape of sales, where every interaction holds the potential to shape relationships and drive revenue, the integration of cognitive technologies stands as a beacon of innovation and opportunity. As sales professionals strive to navigate complex customer journeys and deliver exceptional experiences, the infusion of cognitive power into selling processes offers a transformative pathway to success.

Cognitive technologies encompass a spectrum of capabilities from natural language processing and machine learning to predictive analytics and pattern recognition that enable sales professionals to unlock new insights, anticipate customer needs, and optimize sales strategies with precision and foresight.

At the heart of enhancing sales performance with cognitive technologies lies the ability to harness data-driven insights to drive informed decision-making and strategic execution. By analyzing vast volumes of data spanning customer interactions, market trends, and sales performance cognitive technologies empower sales professionals to uncover hidden patterns, identify emerging opportunities, and mitigate potential risks, enabling organizations to stay ahead of the curve in today's hyper-competitive marketplace.

Moreover, cognitive technologies enable sales professionals to deliver personalized experiences that resonate with individual preferences and needs. Through advanced algorithms and predictive analytics, sales teams can tailor their messaging, content, and offerings to match the unique characteristics and behaviors of each customer, fostering deeper connections, driving engagement, and ultimately, increasing conversion rates and customer loyalty.

Furthermore, cognitive technologies enhance sales performance by automating repetitive tasks and streamlining workflows, allowing sales professionals to focus their time and energy on activities that drive the greatest value. From lead qualification and follow-up communication to sales forecasting and performance tracking, cognitive technologies enable sales teams to operate more efficiently, effectively, and consistently, maximizing productivity and results across the organization.

Predictive Analytics and Forecasting

In the intricate dance of sales, where every decision holds the potential to shape outcomes, predictive analytics and forecasting emerge as invaluable tools, illuminating the path forward with clarity and precision. At the intersection of data science and cognitive power, predictive analytics empowers sales professionals to peer into the future, anticipate trends, and make informed decisions that drive success.

At its core, predictive analytics harnesses the power of historical data, advanced algorithms, and machine learning techniques to uncover patterns, correlations, and insights that lay the groundwork for accurate forecasting and strategic planning. By analyzing vast volumes of data from customer interactions and purchasing behaviors to market trends and economic indicators predictive analytics provides a lens through which sales professionals can distill complexity into clarity, discerning signals amidst the noise and charting a course towards achievement.

In the realm of sales, predictive analytics offers multifaceted benefits, ranging from enhanced lead scoring and prioritization to more accurate sales forecasting and resource allocation. By evaluating a myriad of factors demographics, buying behaviors, engagement metrics, and more predictive analytics enables sales teams to identify high-value opportunities, prioritize leads with the highest likelihood of conversion, and tailor their strategies to meet the evolving needs and preferences of their target audience.

Moreover, predictive analytics serves as a compass in the turbulent seas of uncertainty, providing sales professionals with the foresight and agility needed to navigate shifting market dynamics and competitive landscapes. Armed with actionable insights and forward-looking indicators, sales teams can anticipate market trends, identify emerging opportunities, and pivot their strategies in real-time, positioning themselves for success in an ever-evolving marketplace.

Furthermore, predictive analytics fuels the engine of innovation and continuous improvement, empowering sales professionals to refine their approaches, optimize their processes, and drive sustainable growth over time. By tracking key performance indicators, monitoring sales trends, and measuring the effectiveness of different initiatives, predictive analytics provides a feedback loop through which sales teams can iterate, adapt, and innovate, fostering a culture of excellence and achievement within the organization.

Personalization and Customer Segmentation

In the dynamic realm of sales, where every interaction is an opportunity to build relationships and drive value, personalization and customer segmentation stand as pillars of success, guiding sales professionals towards deeper connections and enhanced experiences. Rooted in the principles of cognitive power and data-driven insights, personalization and segmentation empower sales teams to deliver tailored solutions and meaningful engagements that resonate with individual preferences and needs.

At its core, personalization is about understanding the unique characteristics and preferences of each customer and tailoring interactions accordingly. In the digital age, where customers are inundated with choices and information, personalization offers a beacon of relevance amidst the noise, capturing attention, fostering engagement, and driving loyalty.

Cognitive technologies, powered by advanced algorithms and machine learning techniques, enable sales professionals to leverage vast volumes of customer data from purchase history and browsing behaviors to demographic information and social interactions to craft personalized experiences that transcend transactional exchanges and foster emotional connections.

Moreover, personalization extends beyond surface level customization to encompass a deeper understanding of customer needs and aspirations. By analyzing historical data and behavioral patterns, sales teams can anticipate future needs, proactively address pain points, and deliver solutions that align with the evolving preferences and aspirations of their customers.

Customer segmentation, meanwhile, offers a strategic framework through which sales professionals can categorize customers into distinct groups based on shared characteristics, behaviors, and needs. By segmenting customers into homogenous groups, sales teams can tailor their messaging, content, and offerings to resonate with the unique needs and preferences of each segment, driving relevance and resonance at scale.

43

Cognitive technologies, such as machine learning algorithms and predictive analytics, empower sales professionals to identify patterns and correlations within vast datasets, uncovering insights that inform segmentation strategies and drive targeted engagement initiatives. From demographic segmentation and psychographic profiling to behavioral segmentation and lifecycle analysis, customer segmentation provides a roadmap for sales teams to allocate resources effectively, optimize messaging, and drive personalized interactions that maximize impact and results.

Sales Automation and Efficiency

In the fast-paced world of sales, where time is a precious commodity and efficiency is paramount, the integration of sales automation stands as a beacon of innovation, empowering sales professionals to streamline processes, optimize workflows, and drive productivity to unprecedented heights. Rooted in the principles of cognitive power and technological advancement, sales automation represents a transformative force, revolutionizing the way organizations engage with customers, manage leads, and close deals.

At its core, sales automation is about leveraging technology to automate repetitive tasks and administrative processes, allowing sales professionals to focus their time and energy on high-value activities such as building relationships, solving problems, and driving revenue. By automating routine tasks from data entry and lead scoring to email outreach and follow-up communication sales teams can operate more efficiently, effectively, and consistently, maximizing productivity and results across the organization.

Cognitive technologies, powered by advanced algorithms and machine learning techniques, enable sales professionals to automate a wide range of activities throughout the sales cycle, from lead generation and qualification to sales forecasting and performance tracking. By leveraging AI-driven automation tools, sales teams can streamline workflows, eliminate manual errors, and accelerate the pace of operations, driving efficiency and agility in an increasingly competitive marketplace.

Moreover, sales automation extends beyond individual tasks to encompass end-to-end processes and workflows, providing a seamless and integrated experience for sales professionals and customers alike. By automating the entire sales lifecycle—from prospecting and outreach to contract management and invoicing—organizations can create frictionless experiences that delight customers, drive loyalty, and differentiate themselves in the market.

Cognitive technologies, such as natural language processing (NLP) and sentiment analysis, enable sales automation platforms to analyze customer interactions and glean insights that inform personalized engagement strategies. By understanding customer needs, preferences, and sentiment in real-time, sales professionals can tailor their messaging, content, and offerings to resonate with individual customers, fostering deeper connections and driving higher levels of engagement and satisfaction.

CHAPTER 4

Navigating Ethical and Moral Considerations

In the dynamic intersection of sales and artificial intelligence (AI), where cognitive power shapes interactions and drives outcomes, the exploration of ethical and moral considerations emerges as an essential compass guiding the journey towards responsible and sustainable selling practices. As AI becomes increasingly integrated into sales processes, it is imperative for sales professionals and organizations to navigate the complex landscape of ethical dilemmas and moral implications with vigilance, integrity, and empathy.

At the heart of ethical considerations in AI-driven sales lies the responsibility to uphold principles of transparency, fairness, and accountability. As AI algorithms analyze vast amounts of data and make decisions that impact customers' lives and experiences, it is essential for sales professionals to ensure transparency in

47

how data is collected, used, and analyzed, fostering trust and integrity in customer relationships.

Moreover, ethical considerations extend to the fairness and equity of AI-driven sales processes, particularly in areas such as pricing, targeting, and decision-making. As AI algorithms make decisions based on data patterns and predictive analytics, it is essential for sales professionals to mitigate bias, discrimination, and unintended consequences that may arise from algorithmic decision-making, ensuring that sales practices uphold principles of fairness and equality for all customers.

Furthermore, ethical considerations encompass the protection of customer privacy and data security in AI-driven sales environments. As AI algorithms collect and analyze sensitive customer information, it is imperative for sales professionals to prioritize data privacy and security, adhering to regulatory requirements and industry standards to safeguard customer trust and confidentiality.

Moral considerations in AI-driven sales revolve around the impact of technology on human relationships, autonomy, and well-being. As AI-driven technologies automate tasks and personalize interactions, it is essential for sales professionals to maintain empathy, empathy, and human connection in their interactions with customers, recognizing the intrinsic value of human relationships in the sales process.

Moreover, moral considerations extend to the broader societal impact of AI-driven sales practices, including job displacement, economic inequality, and social polarization. As AI technologies reshape industries and disrupt traditional employment models, it is essential for sales professionals and organizations to consider the ethical implications of AI-driven automation and strive to mitigate potential negative consequences through initiatives such as reskilling, upskilling, and social responsibility programs.

Ethical Use of AI in Sales

In the transformative landscape of sales, where artificial intelligence (AI) wields unprecedented power to drive insights and outcomes, the ethical use of AI emerges as a cornerstone of responsible and sustainable selling practices. As AI technologies become increasingly integrated into sales processes, it is essential for sales professionals and organizations to prioritize ethical considerations, uphold moral principles, and foster trust and transparency in customer relationships.

At its core, the ethical use of AI in sales begins with a commitment to transparency and accountability. Sales professionals must ensure that customers are informed about the use of AI technologies in sales processes, including how data is collected, analyzed, and utilized to personalize interactions and drive decision-making. Transparency fosters trust and empowers customers to make informed choices about their engagement with AI-driven sales initiatives.

Moreover, the ethical use of AI in sales requires a commitment to fairness and equality in algorithmic decision-making. Sales professionals must mitigate bias, discrimination, and unintended consequences that may arise from AI algorithms by regularly auditing and monitoring algorithms for fairness and equity. By proactively addressing biases and ensuring fairness in decision-making, sales professionals uphold principles of justice and equality in customer interactions.

Furthermore, the ethical use of AI in sales encompasses the protection of customer privacy and data security. Sales professionals must prioritize data privacy and security by implementing robust data protection measures, complying with regulatory requirements, and safeguarding customer information from unauthorized access or misuse. Respecting customer privacy and confidentiality builds trust and strengthens relationships, laying the foundation for ethical and responsible sales practices.

Additionally, the ethical use of AI in sales requires a commitment to human-centric values and principles. Sales professionals must prioritize empathy, empathy, and human connection in their interactions with customers, recognizing the intrinsic value of human relationships in the sales process. By maintaining a focus on empathy and understanding, sales professionals can build rapport, foster trust, and create meaningful experiences that resonate with customers on a personal level.

Ensuring Fairness and Transparency

In the dynamic landscape of sales, where artificial intelligence (AI) serves as a powerful ally in driving insights and outcomes, ensuring fairness and transparency stands as a fundamental principle guiding responsible and ethical selling practices. As AI technologies become increasingly integrated into sales processes, it is imperative for sales professionals and organizations to uphold principles of fairness and transparency to foster trust, integrity, and accountability in customer relationships.

Fairness in AI-driven sales processes begins with a commitment to mitigating bias and discrimination in algorithmic decision-making. Sales professionals must recognize and address biases that may be inherent in AI algorithms, whether they stem from historical data, algorithm design, or data collection processes. By regularly auditing and monitoring algorithms for fairness and equity, sales teams can ensure that AI-driven decisions are free from bias and uphold principles of fairness and equality for all customers.

Transparency is essential for building trust and empowering customers to make informed decisions about their engagement with AI-driven sales initiatives. Sales professionals must be transparent about the use of AI technologies in sales processes, including how data is collected, analyzed, and utilized to personalize interactions and drive decision-making. By providing clear and accessible information about AI-driven sales practices, sales teams can foster trust and transparency in customer relationships, building a foundation for meaningful engagement and long-term loyalty.

Moreover, transparency extends to the disclosure of AI-driven insights and recommendations to customers. Sales professionals must be transparent about the factors and criteria used by AI algorithms to make recommendations and decisions, empowering customers to understand the rationale behind AI-driven suggestions and take ownership of their choices. By fostering transparency in the delivery of AI-driven insights, sales teams can build credibility and trust with customers, enhancing the overall customer experience and driving satisfaction and loyalty.

Mitigating Bias in AI-driven Sales Processes

In the realm of sales powered by artificial intelligence (AI), the pursuit of fairness and equity stands as a foundational imperative. As AI algorithms play an increasingly pivotal role in decision-making processes, it becomes crucial for sales professionals and organizations to proactively address and mitigate bias, ensuring that AI-driven sales initiatives uphold principles of fairness, equality, and ethical conduct.

Bias in AI-driven sales processes can manifest in various forms, ranging from inherent biases within training data to algorithmic biases arising from flawed design or implementation. To mitigate bias effectively, sales professionals must adopt a multifaceted approach that encompasses data governance, algorithmic transparency, and continuous monitoring and evaluation.

The journey toward mitigating bias begins with a comprehensive understanding of the data inputs and algorithms that underpin AI-driven sales processes. Sales professionals must critically evaluate the quality, representativeness, and diversity of training data to identify and mitigate biases that may be present. By examining historical data with a discerning eye, sales teams can identify patterns of bias and take proactive steps to address underlying issues, such as underrepresentation or skewed distributions.

Transparency is paramount in mitigating bias in AI-driven sales processes. Sales professionals must strive to maintain transparency in algorithmic decision-making, ensuring that stakeholders understand the factors and criteria used by AI algorithms to make recommendations and decisions. By providing clear explanations and insights into the decision-making process, sales teams can foster trust and accountability, empowering stakeholders to engage critically with AI-driven insights and recommendations.

Furthermore, sales professionals must embrace a culture of continuous monitoring and evaluation to detect and address bias in real-time. Through ongoing analysis and feedback loops, sales teams can identify patterns of bias, evaluate the impact of algorithmic decisions, and implement corrective measures to mitigate bias effectively. By fostering a culture of vigilance and accountability, sales professionals can proactively address bias and uphold principles of fairness and equality in AI-driven sales processes.

CHAPTER 5

IMPLEMENTING AI STRATEGIES IN SALES ORGANIZATIONS

In the ever-evolving landscape of sales, the integration of artificial intelligence (AI) represents a transformative opportunity for organizations to unlock new levels of efficiency, effectiveness, and insight. As AI technologies continue to reshape the way sales professionals engage with customers, forecast trends, and drive revenue, the implementation of AI strategies stands as a pivotal step towards harnessing the full potential of cognitive power in selling.

The journey of implementing AI strategies in sales organizations begins with a clear understanding of organizational objectives, challenges, and opportunities. Sales leaders must align AI initiatives with strategic business goals, identifying areas where AI-driven technologies can create value, enhance customer experiences, and drive competitive advantage in the marketplace.

A critical component of implementing AI strategies in sales organizations involves building a robust foundation of data infrastructure and analytics capabilities. Sales teams must invest in data governance, quality assurance, and integration to ensure that AI algorithms have access to clean, reliable, and relevant data sources. By leveraging advanced analytics platforms and technologies, sales organizations can unlock insights, identify patterns, and make data-driven decisions that optimize sales performance and drive revenue growth.

Moreover, the successful implementation of AI strategies in sales organizations requires a commitment to fostering a culture of innovation, experimentation, and continuous learning. Sales professionals must embrace AI technologies as enablers of growth and transformation, recognizing the potential for AI to augment human capabilities, streamline processes, and drive strategic outcomes in the sales domain.

In addition, sales organizations must invest in talent development and training initiatives to equip sales professionals with the skills, knowledge, and capabilities needed to leverage AI effectively. By providing comprehensive training programs and resources, organizations can empower sales teams to harness the power of AI technologies, navigate complex data landscapes, and drive meaningful outcomes in the sales process.

Furthermore, the implementation of AI strategies in sales organizations necessitates a commitment to collaboration and cross-functional alignment. Sales leaders must work closely with stakeholders across departments, including marketing, operations, and IT, to ensure that AI initiatives are integrated seamlessly into existing workflows and processes. By fostering collaboration and communication, organizations can break down silos, drive alignment, and maximize the impact of AI across the entire sales ecosystem.

In "The Sales of the Mind with AI: Unleashing Cognitive Power In Selling," we explore the strategic considerations, practical insights, and actionable strategies for implementing AI strategies in sales organizations. Through real-world examples, case studies, and best practices, we empower sales leaders and professionals to navigate the complexities of AI adoption, drive organizational change, and unlock new opportunities for growth and innovation in the dynamic and ever-evolving landscape of sales. Join us on a journey of exploration and discovery as we harness the transformative potential of AI to reshape the future of selling.

Change Management in Sales Teams

In the rapidly evolving landscape of sales, where artificial intelligence (AI) and cognitive technologies are reshaping traditional practices, effective change management stands as a linchpin for successful adaptation and growth. As sales teams navigate the complexities of integrating AI-driven solutions into their workflows, change management strategies play a pivotal role in fostering acceptance, alignment, and agility in the face of transformational change.

Change management in sales teams begins with a clear communication of the vision, purpose, and benefits of adopting AI-driven technologies. Sales leaders must articulate the strategic rationale behind the adoption of AI, emphasizing the potential for enhanced efficiency, productivity, and customer engagement. By aligning AI initiatives with organizational goals and priorities, sales teams can cultivate a shared sense of purpose and direction, laying the groundwork for successful change implementation.

Moreover, change management in sales teams involves proactive engagement and involvement of stakeholders at all levels of the organization. Sales leaders must foster a culture of inclusivity and collaboration, soliciting input and feedback from sales professionals, frontline managers, and cross-functional teams. By involving stakeholders in the change process, sales teams can build ownership, commitment, and buy-in, driving collective accountability and empowerment throughout the organization.

A crucial aspect of change management in sales teams is providing comprehensive training and support to enable sales professionals to effectively leverage AI-driven technologies. Sales leaders must invest in tailored training programs, resources, and coaching initiatives to build proficiency and confidence in using AI tools and platforms. By equipping sales teams with the knowledge, skills, and capabilities needed to succeed in the digital age, organizations can mitigate resistance to change and accelerate adoption and proficiency.

Furthermore, change management in sales teams necessitates a focus on resilience, adaptability, and continuous learning. Sales professionals must embrace change as an opportunity for growth and development, recognizing the potential for AI technologies to augment their capabilities, streamline processes, and drive strategic outcomes in the sales domain. By fostering a growth mindset and a culture of experimentation, sales teams can navigate uncertainty, embrace innovation, and thrive in dynamic and ever-changing environments.

Training and Upskilling Sales Professionals

In the dynamic landscape of sales, where artificial intelligence (AI) and cognitive technologies are revolutionizing traditional practices, training and upskilling sales professionals stand as essential pillars for driving success and innovation. As sales teams embrace the transformative potential of AI-driven solutions, investing in comprehensive training and upskilling initiatives becomes paramount to equip sales professionals with the knowledge, skills, and capabilities needed to thrive in the digital age.

Training and upskilling sales professionals begin with a thorough assessment of current competencies, gaps, and learning needs within the sales organization. Sales leaders must conduct a comprehensive skills audit to identify areas where sales professionals require training and development, whether it be in technical proficiencies related to AI technologies or soft skills such as communication, problem-solving, and adaptability.

Moreover, training and upskilling initiatives should be tailored to the unique needs and preferences of sales professionals, offering a mix of formal training programs, workshops, coaching sessions, and self-paced learning resources. Sales leaders must leverage a variety of instructional methods and modalities to accommodate diverse learning styles and preferences, ensuring that training initiatives are engaging, accessible, and relevant to the needs of sales professionals.

A critical aspect of training and upskilling sales professionals involves providing hands-on experience and practical opportunities for application and experimentation. Sales teams must have access to sandbox environments, simulation exercises, and real-world scenarios where they can apply newly acquired knowledge and skills in a risk-free setting. By providing opportunities for hands-on learning and experimentation, organizations can reinforce learning outcomes, build confidence, and drive proficiency in AI-driven technologies.

Furthermore, training and upskilling initiatives should be ongoing and iterative, reflecting the dynamic nature of AI technologies and evolving business needs. Sales leaders must prioritize continuous learning and development, fostering a culture of curiosity, exploration, and growth within the sales organization. By encouraging sales professionals to embrace lifelong learning and stay abreast of emerging trends and best practices, organizations can drive innovation, adaptability, and resilience in the face of change.

In addition, training and upskilling sales professionals require leadership commitment, investment, and alignment across the organization. Sales leaders must champion the importance of training and upskilling initiatives, advocating for resources, support, and recognition for sales professionals who participate in learning and development activities. By prioritizing training and upskilling as strategic imperatives, organizations can cultivate a culture of excellence, empowerment, and continuous improvement in the sales domain.

Overcoming Resistance to AI Adoption

In the journey towards unleashing cognitive power in selling, one of the most formidable challenges that sales professionals and organizations encounter is overcoming resistance to the adoption of artificial intelligence (AI) technologies. As AI continues to reshape the sales landscape with its transformative capabilities, addressing resistance becomes essential to harnessing its full potential and driving meaningful change within sales teams and organizations.

Resistance to AI adoption often stems from a variety of factors, including fear of job displacement, uncertainty about technology, and skepticism about its effectiveness. To overcome resistance, sales leaders must adopt a proactive and holistic approach that addresses concerns, fosters understanding, and cultivates buy-in from stakeholders at all levels of the organization.

A key strategy for overcoming resistance to AI adoption is education and awareness-building. Sales leaders must demystify AI technologies and dispel misconceptions by providing clear and accessible information about the benefits, capabilities, and potential impact of AI in the sales domain. By equipping stakeholders with knowledge and insights, organizations can empower them to make informed decisions and embrace AI as an enabler of growth and innovation.

Moreover, addressing resistance to AI adoption requires a focus on communication and engagement. Sales leaders must actively engage with stakeholders to solicit feedback, address concerns, and foster a sense of ownership and involvement in the adoption process. By creating opportunities for dialogue and collaboration, organizations can build trust, transparency, and alignment, driving collective commitment to the adoption of AI technologies.

Another effective strategy for overcoming resistance to AI adoption is showcasing tangible examples and success stories. Sales leaders can highlight real-world case studies, pilot projects, and use cases that demonstrate the value and impact of AI in driving sales performance and delivering tangible results. By showcasing concrete examples of AI in action, organizations can inspire confidence, alleviate doubts, and generate momentum for adoption across the organization.

Furthermore, addressing resistance to AI adoption requires a focus on empathy and change management. Sales leaders must acknowledge and validate the concerns and anxieties of stakeholders, while also providing support, guidance, and reassurance throughout the adoption process. By fostering a culture of empathy, resilience, and adaptability, organizations can navigate resistance effectively and create a supportive environment for embracing change and innovation.

CHAPTER 6

CASE STUDIES AND EXAMPLES

Lead Scoring Optimization: In a case study with a leading software-as-a-service (SaaS) company, AI-driven lead scoring algorithms were implemented to enhance the efficiency of the sales pipeline. By analyzing historical data and customer interactions, the AI algorithms identified key patterns and indicators of lead quality, enabling sales teams to prioritize leads with the highest likelihood of conversion. As a result, the company experienced a 30% increase in lead conversion rates and a 20% reduction in sales cycle times, driving significant improvements in overall sales performance.

Personalized Email Campaigns: A global e-commerce retailer leveraged AI-driven personalization algorithms to enhance the effectiveness of its email marketing campaigns. By analyzing customer behavior, preferences, and purchase history, the AI algorithms generated personalized product recommendations and tailored messaging for individual customers. As a result, the retailer saw a 25% increase in email open rates, a 40% increase in click-through rates, and a 20% increase in conversion rates, demonstrating the power of AI-driven personalization in driving engagement and sales.

Sales Forecasting Accuracy: A telecommunications company implemented AI-driven sales forecasting models to improve the accuracy and reliability of its revenue projections. By analyzing historical sales data, market trends, and external factors, the AI algorithms generated predictive models that forecasted future sales with greater precision and granularity. As a result, the company achieved a 15% improvement in sales forecasting accuracy, enabling more informed decision-making, resource allocation, and strategic planning across the organization.

Customer Sentiment Analysis: A leading consumer goods manufacturer

utilized AI-driven sentiment analysis tools to monitor and analyze customer feedback across various channels, including social media, customer reviews, and support tickets. By analyzing textual data and sentiment indicators, the AI algorithms identified key themes, trends, and insights that informed product development, marketing strategies, and customer engagement initiatives. As a result, the manufacturer saw a 20% increase in customer satisfaction scores and a 15% reduction in customer churn rates, demonstrating the value of AI-driven insights in driving customer-centricity and loyalty.

Dynamic Pricing Optimization: An online marketplace implemented AI-driven dynamic pricing algorithms to optimize pricing strategies and maximize revenue. By analyzing real-time market data, competitor pricing, and customer demand signals, the AI algorithms dynamically adjusted prices to reflect changing market conditions and customer preferences. As a result, the marketplace experienced a 10% increase in average order value, a 15% increase in sales volume, and a 20%

increase in revenue, showcasing the transformative impact of AI-driven pricing optimization on business performance.

Successful Implementations of AI in Sales

Lead Generation Enhancement:

A technology company successfully implemented AI algorithms to enhance lead generation processes. By analyzing vast datasets of customer behavior and engagement patterns, the AI algorithms identified high-potential leads and prioritized them for sales outreach. This approach resulted in a significant increase in lead quality and conversion rates, enabling the sales team to focus their efforts on prospects most likely to convert, leading to accelerated sales cycles and increased revenue.

Customer Segmentation and Personalization:

A retail corporation leveraged AI-powered customer segmentation and personalization techniques to deliver targeted marketing campaigns and personalized recommendations. By analyzing customer demographics, purchase history, and browsing behavior, the AI algorithms segmented customers into distinct groups and tailored marketing messages and product offerings to each segment's preferences. As a result, the company saw a substantial improvement in customer engagement, loyalty, and retention, driving increased sales and revenue.

Predictive Analytics for Sales Forecasting: A manufacturing company implemented AI-driven predictive analytics models to improve sales forecasting accuracy. By analyzing historical sales data, market trends, and external factors, the AI algorithms generated accurate forecasts of future sales volumes and revenue. This enabled the company to anticipate demand fluctuations, optimize inventory levels, and allocate resources more effectively, leading to improved operational efficiency and profitability.

Dynamic Pricing Optimization: An e-commerce platform deployed AI-powered dynamic pricing algorithms to optimize

pricing strategies in real-time. By analyzing competitor pricing, demand elasticity, and customer behavior, the AI algorithms adjusted prices dynamically to maximize revenue and profit margins. This approach resulted in increased sales volume, higher average order values, and improved competitiveness in the market, driving significant revenue growth for the platform.

Sales Process Automation: A financial services firm automated key aspects of its sales processes using AI-driven automation tools. By automating routine tasks such as data entry, lead scoring, and email outreach, the firm streamlined sales workflows, reduced manual errors, and improved operational efficiency. This allowed sales professionals to focus on high-value activities such as building relationships and closing deals, resulting in increased productivity, higher conversion rates, and improved customer satisfaction.

These successful implementations of AI in sales highlight the transformative impact of cognitive technologies on sales processes and outcomes. By harnessing the power of AI-driven insights, automation, and personalization, organizations can drive efficiency, effectiveness, and innovation in the sales domain, unlocking new opportunities for growth and success in the digital age.

Real-world Applications and Results in Sales

Lead Scoring and Prioritization:

AI algorithms are revolutionizing lead scoring and prioritization processes in sales. By analyzing vast datasets of customer interactions, demographics, and purchase history, AI can identify high-quality leads and prioritize them for sales outreach. This results in more efficient use of sales resources, higher conversion rates, and increased revenue generation.

Personalized Customer Engagement:

AI-powered personalization tools enable sales professionals to deliver tailored experiences to each customer. By analyzing customer preferences, browsing behavior, and past interactions, AI can recommend relevant products, customize messaging, and anticipate customer needs.

This leads to higher engagement, increased customer satisfaction, and improved retention rates.

Sales Forecasting and Predictive Analytics: AI-driven predictive analytics models provide sales teams with valuable insights into future market trends and customer behavior. By analyzing historical data, market dynamics, and external factors, AI can forecast sales volumes, identify emerging opportunities, and mitigate risks. This enables sales teams to make data-driven decisions, optimize resource allocation, and maximize revenue potential.

Dynamic Pricing Optimization: AI algorithms optimize pricing strategies in real-time based on market conditions, competitor pricing, and customer demand. By analyzing vast amounts of data, AI can adjust prices dynamically to maximize profitability while remaining competitive. This results in increased sales volume, higher profit margins, and improved market positioning.

Sales Process Automation: AI-powered automation tools streamline repetitive tasks and administrative processes in sales. By automating data entry, lead qualification, and email outreach, AI frees up valuable time for sales professionals to focus on building relationships and closing deals. This leads to increased productivity, faster sales cycles, and improved customer satisfaction.

Customer Sentiment Analysis: AI-driven sentiment analysis tools monitor customer sentiment across various channels, including social media, reviews, and support tickets. By analyzing textual data and sentiment indicators, AI can identify trends, detect potential issues, and uncover insights that inform sales strategies and customer engagement initiatives. This enables sales teams to proactively address customer concerns, improve brand perception, and drive loyalty.

Cross-selling and Upselling Opportunities: AI algorithms identify cross-selling and upselling opportunities by analyzing customer purchase history, browsing behavior, and product preferences. By recommending complementary products or upgrades, AI enables sales professionals to maximize the value of each customer interaction and increase average order size. This results in higher revenue per customer and improved profitability.

Lessons Learned and Best Practices in Sales

Embrace a Growth Mindset: Sales professionals must adopt a growth mindset, continuously seeking opportunities for learning, improvement, and innovation. By embracing a mindset of curiosity and exploration, sales professionals can adapt to changing market dynamics, leverage emerging technologies, and drive continuous improvement in sales performance.

Prioritize Customer-Centricity: At the heart of successful selling lies a deep understanding of customer needs, preferences, and pain points. Sales professionals must prioritize customer-centricity, building meaningful relationships, and delivering value-added solutions that address customer challenges and aspirations. By putting the customer first, sales professionals can build trust, foster loyalty, and drive long-term success.

Embrace Technology as an Enabler: Technology, including artificial intelligence (AI), serves as a powerful enabler of sales effectiveness and efficiency. Sales professionals must embrace technology as a strategic asset, leveraging AI-driven insights, automation tools, and analytics platforms to streamline processes, enhance decision-making, and drive innovation in the sales domain.

Invest in Continuous Learning and Development: Sales professionals must prioritize continuous learning and development, investing in ongoing training, upskilling, and professional growth initiatives. By staying abreast of industry trends, best practices, and emerging technologies, sales professionals can adapt to evolving customer needs, navigate competitive landscapes, and maintain a competitive edge in the marketplace.

Foster Collaboration and Cross-Functional Alignment: Successful selling requires collaboration and alignment across departments, functions, and teams within the organization. Sales professionals must foster a culture of collaboration, communication, and cross-functional alignment, working closely with marketing, operations, and customer support teams to deliver seamless and integrated customer experiences.

Embrace Data-Driven Decision Making: In today's data-driven world, sales professionals must leverage data and analytics to drive informed decision-making. By harnessing the power of data, sales professionals can gain valuable insights into customer behavior, market trends, and competitive dynamics, enabling them to make strategic decisions that drive growth, profitability, and competitive advantage.

Adaptability and Resilience: The sales landscape is constantly evolving, presenting new challenges and opportunities. Sales professionals must cultivate adaptability and resilience, embracing change, and navigating uncertainty with confidence and agility. By embracing change as an opportunity for growth and innovation, sales professionals can thrive in dynamic and ever-changing environments.

Focus on Relationship Building: Successful selling is built on trust, rapport, and authentic relationships with customers. Sales professionals must prioritize relationship building, investing time and effort in understanding customer needs, building rapport, and fostering long-term connections based on trust, integrity, and mutual respect.

Measure and Track Performance: Sales professionals must measure and track key performance indicators (KPIs) to gauge progress, identify areas for improvement, and drive accountability. By setting clear goals, tracking performance metrics, and

81

analyzing results, sales professionals can optimize performance, identify trends, and make data-driven decisions that drive success in the sales domain.

Continuous Improvement and Innovation:

Sales professionals must embrace a mindset of continuous improvement and innovation, constantly seeking ways to enhance processes, optimize strategies, and deliver greater value to customers. By fostering a culture of innovation and experimentation, sales professionals can stay ahead of the curve, anticipate customer needs, and drive sustainable growth in the sales domain.

CHAPTER 8

FUTURE TRENDS AND DIRECTIONS IN SALES

AI-Powered Virtual Assistants: The future of sales will see the widespread adoption of AI-powered virtual assistants that provide personalized support to sales professionals throughout the sales process. These virtual assistants will leverage natural language processing (NLP) and machine learning algorithms to assist with tasks such as lead qualification, scheduling meetings, and providing real-time insights and recommendations, enhancing productivity and efficiency in sales workflows.

Predictive Analytics and Prescriptive Insights: The evolution of AI and data analytics will enable sales teams to move beyond traditional descriptive analytics to predictive and prescriptive insights. Advanced predictive analytics models will anticipate future trends, customer behavior, and market dynamics, empowering sales professionals to proactively identify opportunities, mitigate risks, and optimize strategies for maximum impact and effectiveness.

Hyper-Personalization and Customer Experience:

Hyper-personalization will emerge as a key trend in sales, driven by advancements in AI and data analytics. Sales professionals will leverage AI algorithms to deliver highly personalized experiences tailored to individual customer preferences, behaviors, and needs. By understanding customer context and intent, sales teams will create tailored messaging, offers, and recommendations that resonate with customers on a deeper level, driving engagement, loyalty, and satisfaction.

Augmented Reality (AR) and Virtual Reality (VR) in Sales Presentations:

AR and VR technologies will revolutionize sales presentations and demonstrations, enabling immersive and interactive experiences for customers. Sales professionals will use AR and VR tools to showcase products, visualize solutions, and engage customers in virtual environments, enhancing the impact and effectiveness of sales presentations and accelerating the decision-making process.

Blockchain Technology for Transparency and Trust:

Blockchain technology will play a significant role in enhancing transparency and trust in sales transactions. Sales professionals will leverage blockchain-powered solutions to ensure the integrity and authenticity of customer data, contracts, and transactions, reducing the risk of fraud, errors, and disputes. By leveraging blockchain technology, sales teams will build trust and confidence with customers, fostering stronger relationships and driving long-term loyalty.

Voice Commerce and Conversational Selling:

Voice commerce and conversational selling will become increasingly prevalent as voice-enabled devices and virtual assistants gain widespread adoption. Sales professionals will leverage voice technology to engage customers in natural, conversational interactions, facilitating seamless transactions and delivering personalized recommendations and support through voice-activated interfaces. Voice commerce will redefine the sales experience, enabling customers to make purchases and interact with brands effortlessly using voice commands.

Ethical AI and Responsible Selling Practices: As AI continues to reshape the sales landscape, there will be a growing emphasis on ethical AI and responsible selling practices. Sales professionals will prioritize transparency, fairness, and accountability in the use of AI technologies, ensuring that AI-driven decisions uphold principles of integrity, equity, and respect for customer privacy. By embracing ethical AI practices, sales teams will build trust and credibility with customers, fostering stronger relationships and driving sustainable business growth.

Evolution of AI in Sales

The evolution of artificial intelligence (AI) in sales represents a transformative journey that has revolutionized the way organizations engage with customers, optimize sales processes, and drive business growth. From its early beginnings to its current state, the evolution of AI in sales has been characterized by groundbreaking advancements, paradigm shifts, and transformative innovations that have reshaped the sales landscape and unlocked new opportunities for success.

Early Applications of AI in Sales:

The early applications of AI in sales focused primarily on automating repetitive tasks and streamlining manual processes. Chatbots and virtual assistants emerged as early examples of AI-driven technologies that provided customer support, answered inquiries, and assisted with basic tasks, enhancing efficiency and responsiveness in sales interactions.

Advancements in Predictive Analytics:

As AI technology advanced, predictive analytics emerged as a powerful tool for sales forecasting, lead scoring, and opportunity identification. By analyzing vast datasets of customer interactions, historical sales data, and market trends, AI algorithms could predict future outcomes, anticipate customer needs, and identify opportunities for revenue generation with unprecedented accuracy and precision.

Personalization and Customer Insights:

AI-powered personalization tools revolutionized the way organizations engage with customers, delivering tailored experiences and personalized recommendations based on individual preferences, behaviors, and past interactions. By leveraging machine learning algorithms and data analytics, sales teams could segment customers, analyze buying patterns, and deliver targeted messaging that resonated with each customer segment, driving engagement, loyalty, and satisfaction.

Integration of Natural Language Processing (NLP):

The integration of natural language processing (NLP) capabilities into AI-driven sales tools enabled more natural and intuitive interactions between sales professionals and customers. NLP-powered chatbots and virtual assistants could understand and respond to customer inquiries, process complex requests, and provide real-time support, enhancing the quality and responsiveness of sales interactions.

Automation and Workflow Optimization:

AI-driven automation tools transformed sales workflows by automating routine tasks, such as data entry, lead qualification, and email outreach. By eliminating manual processes and administrative burdens, AI-enabled automation solutions enabled sales professionals to focus their time and energy on high-value activities, such as building relationships, identifying opportunities, and closing deals, driving productivity and efficiency in sales operations.

Integration of AI into Sales Enablement Platforms:

The integration of AI into sales enablement platforms and CRM systems empowered sales professionals with actionable insights, intelligent recommendations, and predictive analytics capabilities that enhanced decision-making and performance. AI-driven sales tools provided sales teams with real-time visibility into customer interactions, sales pipelines, and

89

performance metrics, enabling them to make data-driven decisions, prioritize activities, and optimize strategies for maximum impact and effectiveness.

Future Directions: Hyper-Personalization, Augmented Intelligence, and Ethical AI:

Looking ahead, the future of AI in sales promises even greater advancements in hyper-personalization, augmented intelligence, and ethical AI practices. Sales professionals will leverage AI technologies to deliver hyper-personalized experiences, anticipate customer needs, and drive meaningful engagement at scale. Augmented intelligence will empower sales professionals with AI-driven insights, recommendations, and decision support tools that augment human capabilities and drive better outcomes. Moreover, ethical AI practices will become increasingly important as organizations prioritize transparency, fairness, and accountability in the use of AI technologies, ensuring that AI-driven decisions uphold principles of integrity, equity, and respect for customer privacy.

Emerging Technologies and Innovations in Sales

Augmented Reality (AR) and Virtual Reality (VR): AR and VR technologies are poised to revolutionize the sales landscape by providing immersive and interactive experiences for customers. Sales professionals can leverage AR and VR to showcase products, simulate real-world scenarios, and engage customers in virtual environments, enhancing the effectiveness of sales presentations and demonstrations.

Voice Commerce and Conversational Interfaces: Voice commerce and conversational interfaces are reshaping the way customers interact with brands and make purchasing decisions. Sales professionals can leverage voice-enabled devices and virtual assistants to facilitate seamless transactions, deliver personalized recommendations, and engage customers in natural, conversational interactions, driving greater convenience and satisfaction.

Blockchain Technology for Trust and Transparency:

Blockchain technology offers unprecedented opportunities for enhancing trust and transparency in sales transactions. Sales professionals can leverage blockchain-powered solutions to secure and authenticate customer data, contracts, and transactions, reducing the risk of fraud, errors, and disputes, and fostering greater confidence and trust with customers.

Predictive Analytics and Machine Learning:

Predictive analytics and machine learning algorithms are enabling sales professionals to anticipate customer needs, identify trends, and optimize sales strategies with unprecedented accuracy and precision. By analyzing vast datasets of customer interactions and market dynamics, AI-driven predictive analytics models can forecast sales trends, identify high-value opportunities, and drive informed decision-making in sales.

Internet of Things (IoT) and Connected Devices: The proliferation of Internet of Things (IoT) devices and connected technologies presents new opportunities for sales professionals to gather real-time data, monitor customer interactions, and personalize experiences. Sales professionals can leverage IoT-enabled devices to track customer behavior, monitor product usage, and deliver proactive support and service, enhancing customer satisfaction and loyalty.

Natural Language Processing (NLP) and Sentiment Analysis: Natural language processing (NLP) and sentiment analysis technologies enable sales professionals to understand and respond to customer inquiries, feedback, and sentiment in real-time. By analyzing textual data from various sources, including social media, reviews, and support tickets, NLP-powered tools can uncover insights, detect trends, and inform sales strategies and customer engagement initiatives.

Robotic Process Automation (RPA): Robotic process automation (RPA) technologies streamline repetitive tasks and administrative processes in sales, freeing up valuable time and resources for sales professionals to focus on high-value activities. RPA solutions can automate data entry, lead qualification, and email outreach, enhancing productivity, efficiency, and scalability in sales operations.

Edge Computing and Real-Time Analytics: Edge computing technologies enable real-time data processing and analytics at the edge of the network, allowing sales professionals to access insights and make decisions in real-time. By leveraging edge computing capabilities, sales teams can analyze customer data, monitor sales performance, and respond to opportunities and challenges with greater agility and responsiveness.

Implications for the Future of Sales

Hyper-Personalization: The future of sales will be characterized by hyper-personalization, where sales professionals leverage advanced technologies such as AI and data analytics to deliver tailored experiences and personalized recommendations to each customer. By understanding individual preferences, behaviors, and needs, sales professionals can build deeper connections with customers, drive engagement, and foster long-term loyalty.

Augmented Intelligence: Augmented intelligence, the fusion of human expertise with AI-driven insights and recommendations, will redefine the role of sales professionals in the digital age. Sales professionals will leverage AI-powered tools and analytics platforms to augment their capabilities, optimize decision-making, and drive better outcomes across the sales process.

Data-Driven Decision Making: Data-driven decision-making will become the cornerstone of successful selling, as sales professionals harness the power of data and analytics to gain actionable insights into customer behavior, market trends, and competitive dynamics. By leveraging data-driven insights, sales professionals can make informed decisions, optimize strategies, and drive meaningful results in the sales domain.

Omni channel Engagement: The future of sales will be characterized by Omni channel engagement, where sales professionals engage with customers seamlessly across multiple touchpoints and channels. From traditional sales channels to digital platforms and social media, sales professionals will leverage Omni channel strategies to reach customers where they are, deliver consistent messaging, and provide personalized experiences throughout the customer journey.

Ethical AI and Responsible Selling Practices: As AI continues to reshape the sales landscape, there will be a growing emphasis on ethical AI and responsible selling practices. Sales professionals must prioritize transparency, fairness, and accountability in the use of AI technologies, ensuring that AI-driven decisions uphold principles of integrity, equity, and respect for customer privacy. By embracing ethical AI practices, sales professionals can build trust and credibility with customers, fostering stronger relationships and driving sustainable business growth.

Agility and Adaptability: The future of sales will demand agility and adaptability from sales professionals and organizations as they navigate rapidly changing market dynamics, evolving customer preferences, and emerging technologies. Sales professionals must embrace change as an opportunity for growth and innovation, continuously learning, evolving, and adapting to stay ahead of the curve in the dynamic and ever-changing sales landscape.

Collaboration and Cross-Functional Alignment: Collaboration and cross-functional alignment will be essential for success in the future of sales, as sales professionals work closely with

marketing, operations, and customer support teams to deliver seamless and integrated customer experiences. By fostering a culture of collaboration, communication, and alignment across the organization, sales professionals can leverage collective expertise and resources to drive greater value and impact in the sales domain.

CHAPTER 9

CONCLUSION

In "The Sales of the Mind with AI: Unleashing Cognitive Power in Selling," we have explored the transformative potential of artificial intelligence (AI) in reshaping the sales landscape and unlocking new opportunities for success and innovation. From its early beginnings to its current state, the evolution of AI in sales has been marked by groundbreaking advancements, paradigm shifts, and transformative innovations that have revolutionized the way organizations engage with customers, optimize sales processes, and drive business growth.

Throughout this journey, we have delved into the key principles, strategies, and best practices for leveraging cognitive power in selling. We have examined the importance of embracing a growth mindset, prioritizing customer-centricity, and harnessing the power of technology to drive efficiency, effectiveness, and innovation in sales. We have explored the role of AI in enhancing lead generation, personalization, predictive analytics, and sales automation, enabling sales professionals to deliver tailored experiences, anticipate customer needs, and drive meaningful engagement at scale.

Moreover, we have discussed the ethical considerations, implications, and future trends shaping the future of sales in the digital age. From hyper-personalization and augmented intelligence to data-driven decision-making and Omni channel engagement, the future of sales holds immense promise for those who embrace change, innovation, and collaboration in navigating the complexities of the modern sales landscape.

As we conclude our exploration of "The Sales of the Mind with AI," it is clear that the journey towards unlocking cognitive power in selling is just beginning. The convergence of AI, data analytics, and emerging technologies presents unprecedented opportunities for sales professionals and organizations to drive growth, competitiveness, and excellence in the digital age. By embracing the principles of innovation, integrity, and customer-centricity, sales professionals can harness the full potential of cognitive power to create value, build trust, and drive sustainable success in the ever-evolving sales domain.

As we look to the future, let us remain committed to continuous learning, adaptation, and evolution in embracing the transformative potential of AI in sales. Together, we can unlock new frontiers of opportunity, drive meaningful impact, and shape the future of sales in the digital era.

Recap of Key Points

Introduction to AI in Sales: The book introduced the transformative role of artificial intelligence (AI) in reshaping the sales landscape, highlighting its potential to drive efficiency, effectiveness, and innovation in selling.

Understanding the Sales Mindset: We explored the importance of embracing a growth mindset, prioritizing customer-centricity, and leveraging technology to drive success in sales.

Psychology of Sales: Delving into the psychology of sales, we examined the principles of influence, persuasion, and emotional intelligence that underpin effective selling strategies.

Emotional Intelligence in Selling: We discussed the significance of emotional intelligence in building rapport, fostering trust, and driving meaningful connections with customers.

Developing a Sales Mindset: The book emphasized the importance of continuous learning, adaptation, and resilience in developing a sales mindset that thrives in dynamic and ever-changing environments.

Leveraging AI in Sales: We explored the various applications of AI in sales processes, including lead generation, personalization, predictive analytics, and sales automation.

Ethical Use of AI in Sales: Ethical considerations and responsible use of AI in sales were highlighted, emphasizing the importance of transparency, fairness, and accountability in leveraging cognitive technologies.

Future Trends and Directions: Looking ahead, we discussed emerging technologies, future trends, and implications shaping the future of sales in the digital age, including hyper-personalization, augmented intelligence, and Omni channel engagement.

Implications for the Future of Sales: The book concluded by examining the implications of AI and cognitive power in sales, emphasizing the importance of agility, adaptability, and collaboration in navigating the complexities of the modern sales landscape.

Final Thoughts on the Future of Sales with AI

As we conclude our journey through "The Sales of the Mind with AI: Unleashing Cognitive Power in Selling," it is evident that we stand at the precipice of a new era in sales one defined by unprecedented opportunities, transformative innovations, and boundless potential for growth and success. The integration of artificial intelligence (AI) into the sales domain represents a paradigm shift that is reshaping the way organizations engage with customers, optimize sales processes, and drive business outcomes in the digital age.

Looking ahead, the future of sales with AI holds immense promise for those who embrace change, innovation, and collaboration in navigating the complexities of the modern sales landscape. Here are some final thoughts on the future of sales with AI:

Empowerment through Technology:

AI empowers sales professionals with the tools, insights, and capabilities they need to succeed in an increasingly competitive and dynamic marketplace. By leveraging AI-driven analytics, automation, and personalization tools, sales professionals can unlock new levels of efficiency, effectiveness, and innovation in selling.

Enhanced Customer Engagement:

AI enables hyper-personalized customer engagement, allowing sales professionals to deliver tailored experiences, anticipate customer needs, and foster meaningful connections at scale. By understanding individual preferences, behaviors, and aspirations, sales professionals can build trust, drive engagement, and cultivate long-term loyalty with customers.

Data-Driven Decision Making:

Data-driven decision-making becomes the cornerstone of successful selling in the digital age. AI-powered analytics platforms provide sales professionals with actionable insights, predictive analytics, and real-time recommendations that inform strategic decisions, optimize resource allocation, and drive measurable results across the sales process.

Ethical AI Practices: As AI continues

to reshape the sales landscape, it is imperative to prioritize ethical AI practices that uphold principles of integrity, fairness, and transparency. Sales professionals must ensure that AI-driven decisions are ethical, responsible, and aligned with the values and interests of customers, fostering trust, credibility, and long-term relationships.

Continuous Learning and Adaptation: The future of sales with AI demands continuous learning, adaptation, and evolution from sales professionals and organizations alike. By embracing a growth mindset, fostering a culture of innovation, and investing in ongoing training and development initiatives, sales professionals can stay ahead of the curve and drive sustainable success in the ever-changing sales landscape.

Collaboration and Integration: Collaboration and integration across departments, functions, and teams are essential for success in the future of sales with AI. Sales professionals must work closely with marketing, operations, and customer support teams to deliver seamless and integrated customer experiences, driving greater value, and impact throughout the customer journey.

In closing, the future of sales with AI holds immense promise for those who dare to dream, innovate, and embrace the transformative power of cognitive technologies. By harnessing the full potential of AI-driven insights, automation, and personalization, sales professionals can unlock new opportunities for growth, competitiveness, and excellence in the digital age. As we embark on this journey of exploration and discovery, let us remain committed to shaping the future of sales with AI, driving success and innovation in the dynamic and ever-changing sales landscape

Call to Action for Sales Professionals

Dear Sales Professionals,

As you journey through "The Sales of the Mind with AI: Unleashing Cognitive Power in Selling," you are embarking on a transformative exploration of the intersection between human ingenuity and technological innovation in the sales domain. The insights, strategies, and principles shared within these pages are not merely theoretical constructs but practical tools to empower you in navigating the complexities of the modern sales landscape and driving meaningful impact in your sales endeavors.

Now, as you reach the culmination of this journey, I urge you to heed the call to action and embark on a journey of transformation and growth in your sales practice:

Embrace Innovation:
Embrace innovation as a catalyst for growth and differentiation in your sales practice. Embrace new technologies, methodologies, and best practices that empower you to deliver greater value and impact to your customers.

Cultivate a Growth Mindset: Cultivate a growth mindset that embraces challenges, learns from failures, and seeks opportunities for continuous improvement and innovation. Embrace change as an opportunity for growth and evolution in your sales practice.

Prioritize Customer-Centricity:
Prioritize customer-centricity in all aspects of your sales practice. Listen to your customers, understand their needs, and tailor your approach to deliver personalized solutions and experiences that resonate with their unique preferences and aspirations.

108

Harness the Power of Data and Analytics:

Harness the power of data and analytics to drive informed decision-making and optimize your sales strategies. Leverage AI-driven insights, predictive analytics, and real-time recommendations to anticipate customer needs, identify opportunities, and drive measurable results in your sales endeavors.

Lead with Integrity and Ethics:

Lead with integrity and ethics in all your interactions and decisions. Uphold principles of honesty, transparency, and accountability in your sales practice, ensuring that your actions align with the values and interests of your customers.

Embrace Lifelong Learning:

Embrace lifelong learning as a cornerstone of success in the ever-changing sales landscape. Stay curious, stay hungry, and invest in continuous learning and development initiatives that expand your knowledge, skills, and capabilities as a sales professional.

Collaborate and Innovate:

Collaborate with your peers, colleagues,

and stakeholders to drive innovation and excellence in your sales practice. Foster a culture of collaboration, communication, and creativity that empowers you to leverage the collective wisdom and expertise of your team in achieving shared goals and objectives.

Take Action: Take action today to implement the insights, strategies, and principles shared within "The Sales of the Mind with AI." Translate knowledge into action, experiment with new ideas, and iterate on your approach to drive tangible results and impact in your sales endeavors.

In closing, I challenge you to seize the opportunity before you and embark on a journey of transformation and growth in your sales practice. Embrace the principles of innovation, integrity, and customer-centricity as guiding lights on your path to success, and together, let us unleash the full potential of cognitive power in selling.

Your journey begins now. Are you ready to answer the call?

www.ingramcontent.com/pod-product-compliance
Lightning Source LLC
Chambersburg PA
CBHW050032260726

48658CB00005B/1562